Be More Dog

Tips and Tricks for Unlocking Your Paw-tential

Alison Davies
Illustrations by Hanna Melin

quadrille

'The gift which I am sending
you is called a dog, and is in
fact the most PRECIOUS and VALUABLE
possession of mankind.'

Theodorus Gaza

CONTENTS

—

'I have found that when you are deeply troubled, there are things you get from the silent devoted companionship of a dog that you can get from no other source.'

Doris Day

Dogs dash, dogs dart, dogs do.

Whether standing resolutely by your side or bounding with their tribe, whatever a dog does, it does 110 per cent. A dog has heart and is not afraid to use it – to love unreservedly or to face-lick with gumption, everything comes from a deep well of affection and a bond that has stood the test of time.

There is no judgement, no canine favouritism – what they see in you is the best.

You are the pinnacle, the apple of their eye, because dogs look beyond the surface. The shiny wrapping paper doesn't matter, it's what's inside that counts.

A loyal confidant, partner in crime and grime, and lifelong ally, the pooch goes beyond the boundaries of time and place. In folklore it is the saviour of man, guiding lost souls to their resting place, and while some myths cite it as a foreboding presence and an omen of things to come, most see the dog as a symbol of faithfulness and all that is good.

To the Native Americans, white dogs were a sign that fortunes would change for the better, particularly when they appeared in groups of three. A barking mutt was also favourable and meant that crops would flourish. Hecate, the wise Greek Goddess of the Moon, is often seen in the company of a black dog, and some say that only acute canine eyes are clever enough to spy her wandering the earth at night.

'DOGS ARE OUR LINK TO PARADISE. THEY DON'T KNOW EVIL . . . OR JEALOUSY . . . OR DISCONTENT. TO SIT WITH A DOG ON A HILLSIDE ON A GLORIOUS AFTERNOON IS TO BE BACK IN EDEN, WHERE DOING NOTHING WAS NOT BORING . . . IT WAS PEACE.'

Milan Kundera

Superstitions aside, there's a definite whiff of the magical about our puppy pals. Super-sensitive noses can sniff out more than the roses and alert us to danger, disease and the forgotten piece of pork pie that's been lurking at the back of the fridge since Christmas!

Padding every step of the way with us as we journey through life, leading us forwards, lifting our spirits and reminding us to have fun for fun's sake, dogs deliver, always.

It makes sense, then, that these tail-wagging wonders can teach us much, depositing tennis balls, bones and the art of bow-wow zen at our feet in equal amounts.

In the pages of this book you'll find a host of doggy dos and don'ts, tips and tricks to keep you on your toes and leaping with delight. A dose of canine comfort coupled with the simple yet playful pleasures that help to ensure every dog has its day. Be yappy and happy and discover your wag, but most of all wear your heart with pride, keep your pack close by your side and... **BE MORE DOG**!

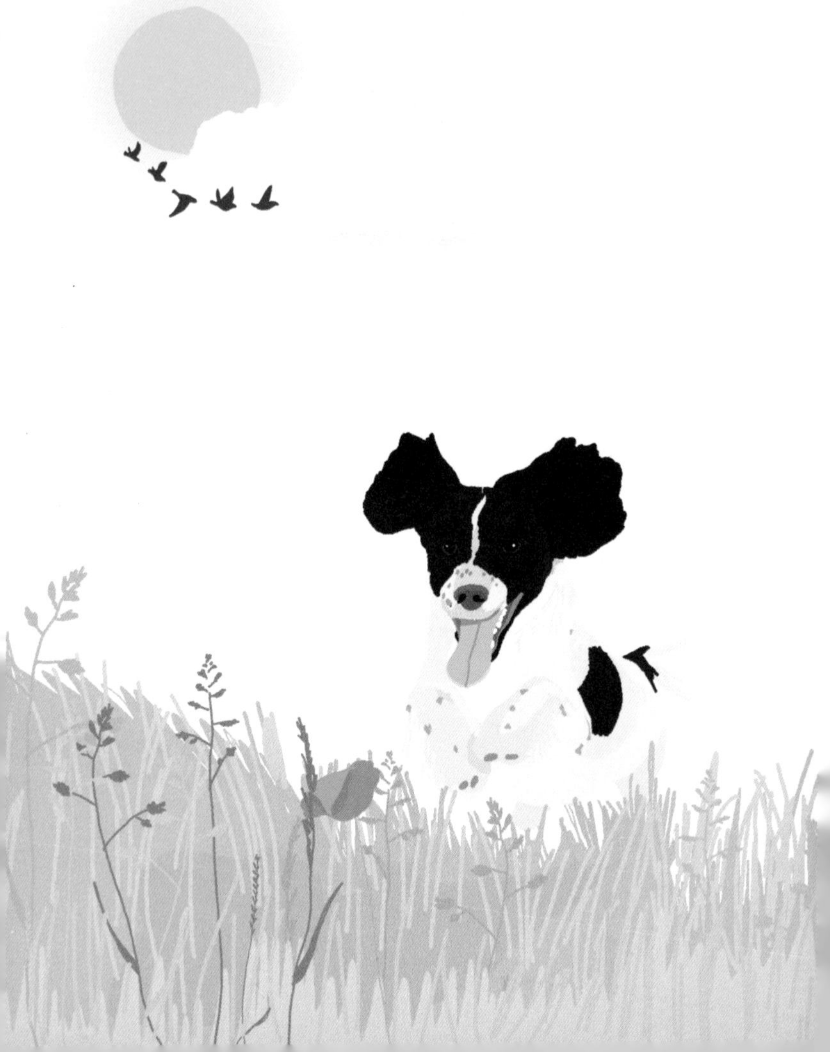

WOOF
IT UP

If dogs could speak, their favourite word would be **YES**, followed by **YES**, and then **YES**, **YES**, **YES**! said with mounting gusto.

They would shout it, sing it and chant it at every opportunity, because **YES** is what they're all about. It's the only word that counts and the only way to be if you're of the canine variety. Known by pooches everywhere as the **YES** factor, the more you have it, the more you want it, because **YES** opens doors. Whether it's a mad dash around the local park or an errant sausage from the barbecue, saying **YES** makes all things possible.

Every dog knows that life is a smorgasbord of tantalising treasures if you open your heart. With fresh eyes they explore, learn, play and embrace the unknown. Such wonders are enough to send them into a tailspin of delight. And while you might ponder at this foolishness, the dog wastes no time searching for a deeper meaning.

LIFE IS FOR DOING — WITHOUT
WORRYING ABOUT THE END RESULT.

The process is where it's at – here, now, in the moment, chasing the elusive tail until you're deliciously dizzy at the sheer exhilaration of it all.

Dogs may appear foolhardy, but they have it sussed.

They know that 'no' is a sad place to be. A place where nothing exciting ever happens. The end of the lead, from which there is no escape. **YES**, on the other hand, is full of possibilities. It's room to breathe and run. Space to race, find, forage and plunder. Our hounds are far from hapless; they might not always have a plan, but who gives a pedigree chum to that?

All pups know you have to woof it up because the destination matters not – the ride is where the fun resides!

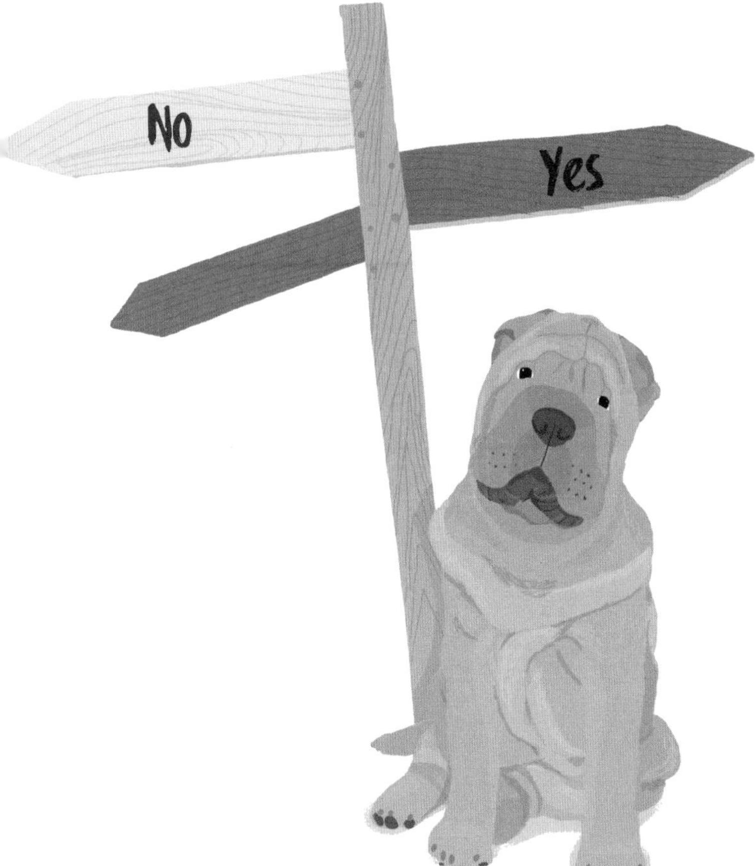
No
Yes

Get the 'Yes' Factor

'Yes' is a simple word, which comes naturally to our canines, but at times it can be hard for us to say it. Don't let fear hold you back. Say 'yes' to new experiences and broaden your horizons by following these dogtastic steps.

STEP ONE – Say 'yes' to yourself.
When you get up in the morning, look in the mirror and say 'Yes!' This is a new day, an empty page and you are top dog.

STEP TWO – Say 'yes' to a new challenge.
Whether it's a routine day at work or your leisure time, make the most of it by embracing challenges that come your way.

Think of a problem as an opportunity to learn, and instead of running for the hills, run towards it as if it's your favourite chew toy!

STEP THREE – Say 'yes' to something you would normally shy away from.
Whether it's an invitation to a party where you don't know anyone, or the opportunity to try out a new skill or activity, count to three, breathe deeply, and in your head say, 'Yes, I can do this!' Then say it for real and mean it.

STEP FOUR – Say 'yes' to helping out.
If you see someone who needs a hand, make a point of offering to help. This kind of 'yes' is the best of all, as there's a purpose to what you're doing, and you'll feel great at the same time.

STEP FIVE – Say 'yes' to your dreams.
Bring to mind any goals or dreams you have. See yourself having achieved your heart's desire. Notice how you look and feel. Say, 'Yes, my dreams are mine!' Be sure to feel excited about the future and what's in store, be it a year, a month or just the next few minutes.

Chase Your Tail

Five paw-pleasing ways to lose yourself in the moment and have some fun.

- Stop what you're doing right now. Breathe and notice how you feel, what you see, hear, smell, taste and feel.

- Recall a moment in time when you had some fun. Bring the memory to mind and relive it. Smile and laugh as you experience it again.

- Pull a funny face in the mirror. Make yourself look as ridiculous as possible for a few seconds every day and enjoy being silly.

- Stick on some upbeat music that makes you want to strut your stuff and go for it!

- Find somewhere you won't be disturbed – a hill, your garden, a cupboard – and shout 'woo hoo!' at the top of your voice.

BE
MORE
DOG

When niggling doubts worm their way into your mind, be more dog and chase them away. Replace worry with action. Take some time out and go walkies! Imagine that with each footfall, you're stamping out the worry. The faster you move, the more fear you clear. Get the blood pumping and increase speed, then when you're out of puff, slow down, relax and enjoy your surroundings.

'My little dog
– a HEARTBEAT at my feet.'

Edith Wharton

Woof it Up

It could be a threadbare slipper, a tennis ball or simply the sight of an open field of freshly mown grass – dogs know there's joy in everything if you look with your heart. Given time, the sagging slipper becomes a thing of beauty, a chew toy with a difference; it is unique to its owner and has layer upon downy layer of fluff to be discovered. The tennis ball goes places one can only wonder at, lifting high in the air and travelling at speed, the perfect opponent for the go-getting pooch. And for the dog who likes to dream, the field becomes a vista of opportunity, a new and enigmatic land where each blade of grass tempts the senses. Perception is everything, and as every good dog will tell you...

If you can't find the fun, be the fun.

'THE GREAT PLEASURE
OF A DOG IS THAT YOU
MAY MAKE A FOOL OF
YOURSELF WITH HIM
AND NOT ONLY WILL HE
NOT SCOLD YOU, BUT HE
WILL MAKE A FOOL OF
HIMSELF TOO.'

Samuel Butler

BE
MORE
DOG

Dogs appreciate what they have and what they are given. In their eager eyes everything is useful and can be made special. Follow suit and take three things, big or small, that have happened today and list the positives. For example, you might have missed the bus to work in the morning, but that gave you the opportunity to catch your breath and chat to someone new at the bus stop.

Give thanks for what you have and what you're given on a regular basis and you'll soon discover that joy is everywhere.

Playtime

Make boredom a thing of the past by shifting your perception. Take a random object and give it new meaning and purpose. Imagine it has secret powers. What would they be? How would you use it? Have fun with this and let your mind wander, creating a scenario in which you might use the object in a different way. Allowing yourself to daydream and be creative might not seem productive, but it's the first step to finding wonder on your doorstep.

DOGGY MANTRAS

DO MORE, WORRY LESS

—

WOOF UP THE VOLUME

—

RUN WITH THE HOUNDS

—

FIND THE FUN, BE THE FUN

—

SAY YES, YES, YES!

'The dog was
created SPECIALLY
FOR CHILDREN. He is
a god of frolic.'

Henry Ward Beecher

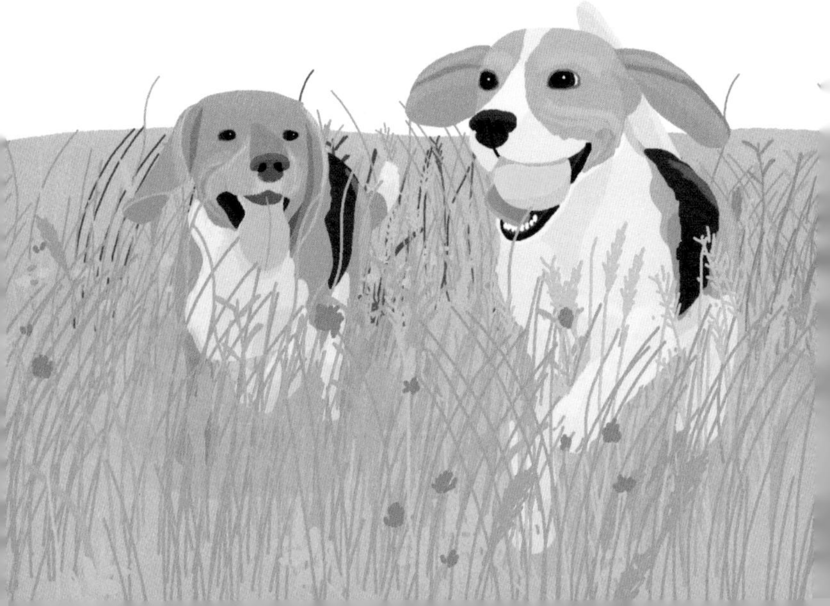

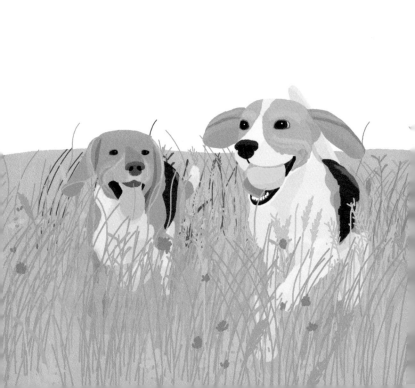

FRIENDS
FOR LIFE

The bond between human and animal is always special, and when it comes to dogs it's as strong as steel.

The chains that bind aren't forged in the fires of Doggy Mount Doom, but they are hardwired into canine DNA, making every pooch, big, small or otherwise, yearn for his tribe. It's about more than being social: it's a way of life. Dogs run together. That's their mode of choice. Each pack takes shape with the leaders at the front. They forage, protect and run ahead of the rest of the group while the most sensitive souls stay at the back, keeping an eye out for trouble.

In the middle you'll find the mediators, always on hand with a cheery yelp and a calm demeanour to smooth things over should tensions arise. It's the natural order of things, and it works because each dog embraces its role and knows its worth. But it doesn't end there.

FELLOWSHIP IS UNIVERSAL.

It doesn't matter who you are; if you're with dog, you're with family.

The weight of such acceptance is what makes our canines thrive, and this is a two-way street. Just as the lead connects you both when you go walkies, so the puppy love flows between you. Whether you pull or they tug, the result is the same: a connection that can withstand anything.

A wet-nosed pal is for life, and sometimes beyond, as little Greyfriars Bobby will attest. This loyal Skye Terrier barked in the face of the grim reaper when his beloved owner passed away in the nineteenth century. According to folklore, he patiently guarded his master's grave in Edinburgh for fourteen years, and these nightly visits became something of a crowd-pleasing spectacle, until Bobby met his end, and hopefully his master, on the other side.

Even kings of legend have the good sense to chum up with a mutt. King Arthur's trusty hound Cavall (also known as Cabal) is famous for killing the supernatural boar Twrch Trwyth. Leaving his paw print on a stone during the legendary hunt, Arthur placed it on the top of a mound of stones to mark the exploits of his faithful friend. The rocky gathering, called Carn Cabal, became a popular landmark, and people came from far and wide to try to steal the sacred stone. Their efforts were in vain, however; Cavall's stone always returned to where his master had laid it.

The fact is, pooches have staying power. Loyal from the tufts of their ears to the jaunty tip of their tail, once they've found their crew, they stick to it like glue.

This makes them the best friend that anyone, man or beast, could ask for.

Create a Fellowship

A sense of fellowship provides strength, stability and huge amounts of happiness, so it's no wonder dogs are always jumping for joy! Are you feeling the love in your life? If you're lacking a pack, or just feel the need to give your closest relationships a boost, then try creating a fellowship, canine style.

STEP ONE
Create time for friends and family. Make a list of those who are important to you and whose time and company you value.

STEP TWO
Look at your diary for the past year and note how much time you've spent with the people that count, from attending special events or meals out, to just hanging with them.

STEP THREE
If you feel you've neglected someone from your list, make changes now. Think of things you can do with that person over the coming months to show them how much they mean to you. Invest time and energy into that relationship and it will blossom.

STEP FOUR

A fellowship works by bringing people together from different walks of life, just as a dog creates its pack with those he spends time with, even if they're not the same species. Plan future dates and social occasions that will bring different groups of friends together.

STEP FIVE

Let everyone find their place in the group. Some will be more sociable and some more sensitive to others' needs. Every person has a role and something they do well. Let them find their position of choice to achieve a happy balance.

'THE POOR DOG,
IN LIFE THE FIRMEST
FRIEND. THE FIRST
TO WELCOME,
FOREMOST TO DEFEND.'

Lord Byron

BE MORE DOG

Dogs share the love daily, whether it's a damp nose against your cheek or a fast and furious facelick. This level of attention might be a step too far for your nearest and dearest, but it's still important to tell them how much they mean to you on a regular basis. Start small with a compliment each day and you'll get into the habit of showing your appreciation more and more.

Run With Your Tribe

- **Whether nose to nose, or any other body part, dogs reach out regularly.**
  Do the same and touch base with friends, family, colleagues and neighbours. Just asking how someone feels is a start, and can be a lifeline for those suffering with loneliness.

- **Dogs play together because they know that fun shared and experienced with friends is always doubled.**
  Do something goal-orientated with your friends or family – anything from training for a marathon to attending an art class will bring you closer as you unite for a common purpose.

- **See the funny side.**
  Make a point of laughing together, often. Being silly in the presence of another is more fun than rolling solo in the mud.

- **Dogs hear when their owner calls, and they listen.**

  They might not understand the lingo but they appreciate the tone and body language, just as they're aware of another dog's proximity and mood from the timbre of its bark. Don't just hear, listen. When someone you know needs to talk, let them.

BE
MORE
DOG

If there's someone you've lost touch with and you'd like to reconnect, picture them standing in front of you. Imagine that you're both holding one end of a long lead, which is gradually shortening, pulling you closer together. Eventually you're face to face.

Picture the pair of you hugging, and as you do the lead dissolves and you're connected heart to heart. Follow this up by getting in touch with this person. You can do this by phone, text, email or letter, whichever form of communication feels most comfortable in the situation.

'WHEN THE MAN WAKED UP HE SAID, "WHAT IS WILD DOG DOING HERE?" AND THE WOMAN SAID, "HIS NAME IS NOT WILD DOG ANY MORE, BUT THE FIRST FRIEND, BECAUSE HE WILL BE OUR FRIEND FOR ALWAYS AND ALWAYS AND ALWAYS."'

Rudyard Kipling

Strengthen Your Connections

You don't have to be canine to form strong bonds with those in your life. Memories are the glue that holds every relationship together.

Find a box you like, or take an old shoe box and decorate it to make it look special. This is going to be your memory box. Fill it with photographs, with treasures from special moments, and mementos of events and occasions.

Make a point of adding to the box every couple of weeks, and remember to pull things out occasionally and relive the fun times!

DOGGY MANTRAS

LOVE IS A TWO-WAY LEAD

—

ALWAYS CHOOSE PEDIGREE CHUMS

—

FACE TO FACE IS HEART TO HEART

—

FUN SHARED IS FUN DOUBLED

—

EMBRACE YOUR MATES

'Money can buy
you a fine dog,
but only LOVE
can make him
WAG his tail.'

Richard Friedman

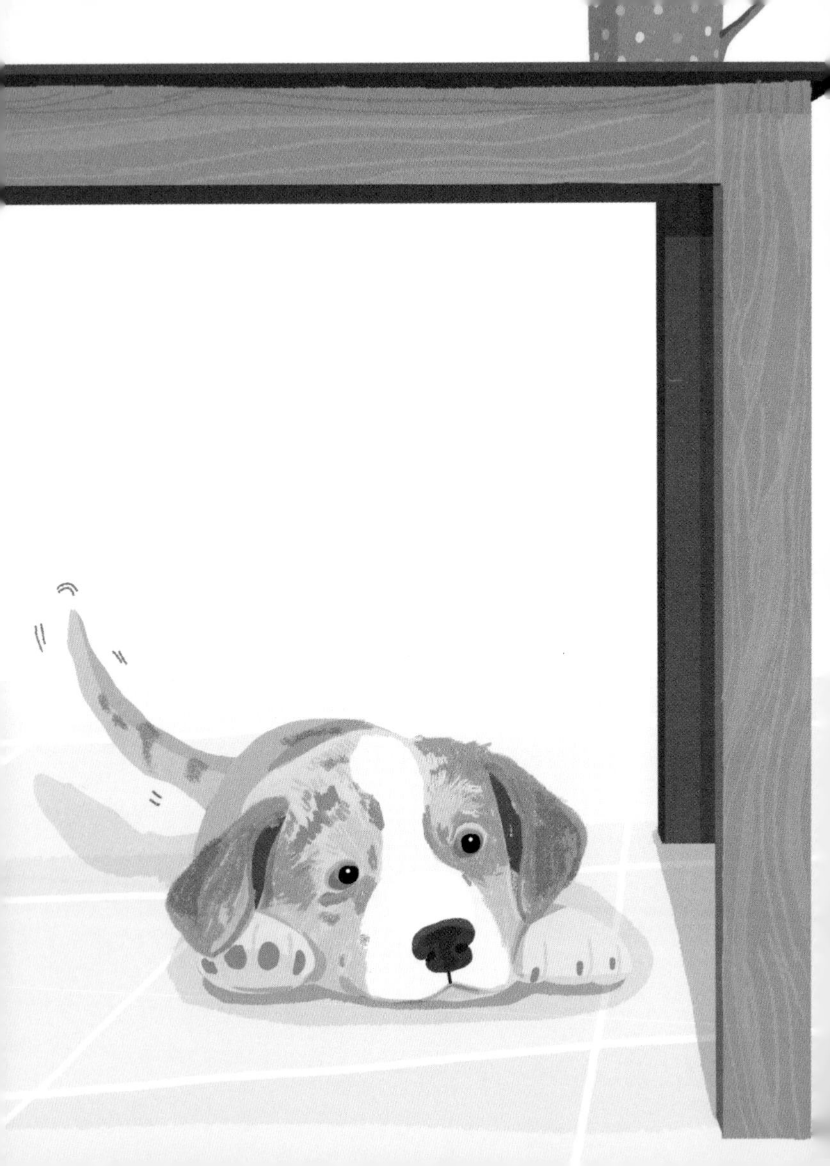

FIND
YOUR WAG

According to the law of dog, there's a silver lining to every scenario if you're willing to sniff it out.

The world is a wagtastically wonderful place when approached with a positive attitude, and there's nothing our canines love more than a chance to use their wag. That said, a dog's tail has a tale of its own to reveal. It's not just a frivolous fur-clad appendage designed to look cute; the tail provides balance, helping dogs to steer and cut corners when bounding at speed, and acting as a rudder in the water.

On the surface then, the tail is a practical tool, but what about the infamous wag? Infectious and undeniably appealing, it spells excitement with a capital E! In the most part, and particularly when it's leaning to the right, the tail wag is a thing of joy, but should it stray to the left, then elation turns to distress. Either way, a wagging tail says, 'Listen up folks!' It's a call to arms, and paws, and any other part that might garner some attention.

Beneath the flurry of movement there's another deeper message: engage with me, engage with life, engage right now.

It's time to get excited. To get your wag on. To look and be the best. Doesn't matter what doggy doings are going down. So you've metaphorically stood in the poop – so what? Shake your leg. Shake your rear end. Move on and smell the sunshine! Incidentally, standing in dog muck may be far from your fragrant cup of tea, but in France it's viewed as good luck, should the deed be done with your left foot.

There's a lesson in everything, so sayeth the pooch. The smell of success is sweet, but the ubiquitous whiff of failure can also lead to a new adventure, an understanding hard won by. When things take a turn for the worst, don't stand with your tail between your legs.

Rise up and recognise you have even more reason to find your wag, then look to the things you can savour, look to the future, and always woof on the bright side of life!

'DOGS ARE WISE.
THEY CRAWL AWAY INTO
A QUIET CORNER AND LICK
THEIR WOUNDS AND DO
NOT REJOIN THE WORLD
UNTIL THEY ARE WHOLE
ONCE MORE.'

Agatha Christie

Locate Your Wag

We like to make things complicated, but dogs seek out simplicity, which is why they have no trouble finding their wag. Practise these steps at the start or finish of every day and unleash your waggle

STEP ONE
Place your hands beneath your belly button, palms down, and focus on your breathing.

STEP TWO
Extend each breath you take by two counts and enjoy the feeling of deep relaxation as it emanates from your belly.

STEP THREE
Smile, even if you don't feel it in your heart. Make it the biggest, brightest smile you can muster, and then continue to breathe deeply.

STEP FOUR
Gently shake your arms and legs, building up speed until you're moving every part of your body and wiggling every muscle. Imagine you're shaking off all your worries and fears.

STEP FIVE
To finish, return to a standing position, breathe deeply and say, 'I am filled with positive energy!'

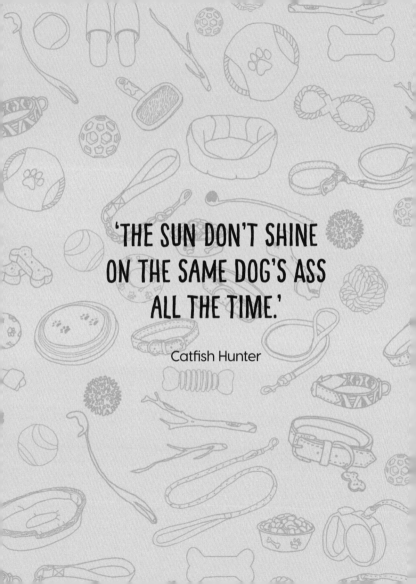

'THE SUN DON'T SHINE
ON THE SAME DOG'S ASS
ALL THE TIME.'

Catfish Hunter

Five reasons to be canine cheerful.

1 **It might be raining outside, but that just means there's more scope to slip and slide.**
OK, so things aren't going your way – maybe it's time to try a new way! Adapt your method, go with it, and enjoy the surprise of doing something different.

2 **You may have lost your favourite ball, but you've had hours of fun trying to find it.**
You haven't reached your goal just yet, but what have you learned on the way? How many new skills have you picked up that you could use in the future? It's not always about the destination – the journey counts too.

3 **The lead restricts you, but it also keeps you safe and close to those you love.**
Daily chores and tasks might seem stifling, but they also remind you of who and what is important, and give you a sense of order and purpose.

4 **There might be bigger, faster pedigree pooches on the block, but they haven't met you yet.**
You may feel you fall short in some way, but you are unique and have your own gifts and talents. Let others love you for you, not for what you think you should be. Every dog has its day and its place in the world.

5 **The Sunday roast appears to be off limits, but it's tantalised your taste buds.**
If something is just out of reach, don't despair. Take the drive you feel and use it to motivate you every day.

'A man may smile
and bid you hail

Yet wish you to
the devil;

But when a GOOD
DOG WAGS HIS TAIL,

You know he's on
the level.'

Anonymous

BE
MORE
DOG

A dog's tail is its anchor, providing balance
and agility. Find your own centre of gravity
and the point from which you can reach in
any direction. Stand with feet hip-width apart,
shoulders back and head tilted upwards. Drop
your weight into the soles of your feet and
bend lightly at the knees. Bounce gradually in
this position and feel the strength and stability
as your weight is supported. Stretch up with
your arms and bend forwards from the waist.
If you can, let your hands rest on your feet
for a few seconds, then unfurl and reach up
to the stars. Straighten your legs and let your
spine lengthen.

Woof on the Bright Side

Want to ensure that every day is filled with sunshine and a hefty dose of delectable treats?

Then keep in mind the doggy mantra **positive paws open doors.** Sounds simple – because it is! Our canines make things easy for us. There's no need for hours of meditation, unless you want to chew that particular bone. Positive paws always have a spring in their step, wherever they're headed. Come rain or shine, whatever the climate, positive paws feel the ground supporting them. They travel forwards with a lightness of touch that makes it look like they're walking on air. You can do the same by repeating this mantra as you walk, talk and play.

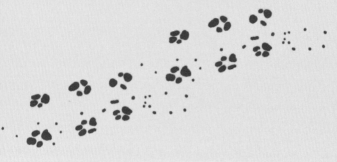

BE
MORE
DOG

Get down and dirty in the mud from time to time. You don't have to roll around in it, unless you really want to – take up a spot of gardening instead, from planting pots to weeding; anything that connects you with the earth will help you feel energised and more positive. Stick your fingers deep in the dirt and feel the damp moisture of the earth clinging to you. Enjoy the sensation of being at one with nature!

DOGGY MANTRAS

POSITIVE PAWS OPEN DOORS
-
EVEN IN MUD, THERE'S JOY TO BE HAD
-
SHAKE IT, FAKE IT, MAKE IT!
-
BE WAGTASTIC AND WONDERFUL
-
EVERY DOG HAS ITS DAY

'Dogs don't RATIONALISE. They don't hold anything against a person. They don't see the outside of a human but the INSIDE OF A HUMAN.'

Cesar Millan

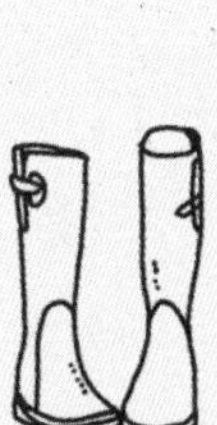

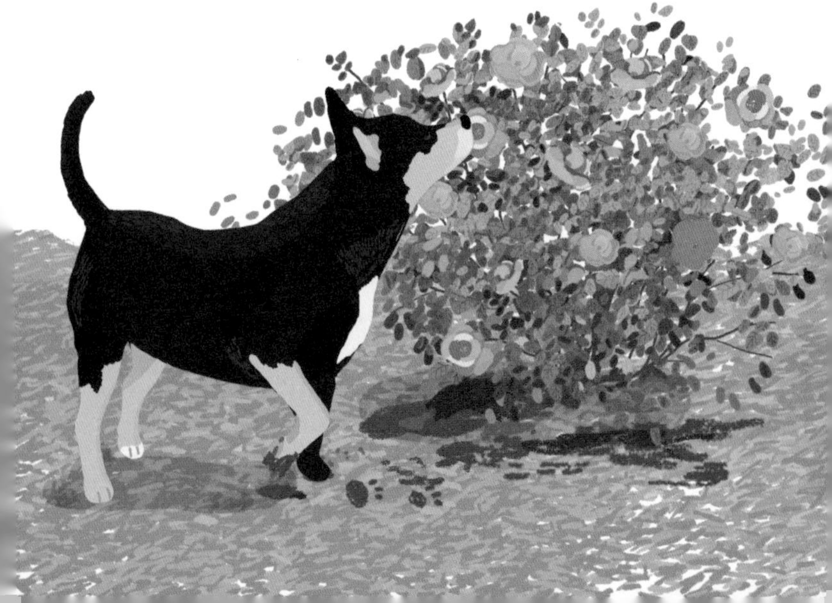

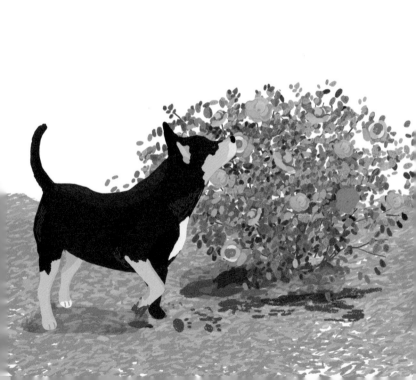

YOUR NOSE KNOWS

A dog's super power resides in his nose. With 300 million scent receptors and a smell centre in the brain up to forty times bigger than our own, it's no surprise that dogs can sniff out just about anything.

It's not about the power of the pong either. Their highly developed sense of smell means that they can identify all the components of a specific aroma, so while the cake in the oven might smell nice to us, a pooch will know exactly what goes into each yummy mouthful. Not only that, he'll probably be able to tell you precisely when it was made and when it will be ready, thanks to his time-travelling nostrils, which can sense odours from the past and those about to be unleashed – no time machine required!

Dogs understand that everything goes with the nose. Fishy whiffs notwithstanding, if something doesn't sit well in its smell, then it's one massive alarm bell. From Scooby-Doo to Lassie, heroic pooches waste no time in using their super schnauzer to save the day, the planet and humankind – and all before morning walkies.

You see, while they have excellent vision, their nose is also 'all-seeing', tracking the fragrant clouds of scent that waft around us. This third eye, strategically placed in the middle of the face, draws in aromas like a funnel – from the stench of disease to a sudden decrease in blood sugar, our mighty mutts are on the case quicker than you can say Sherlock Hounds!

We might not consider the schnozzle a thing of beauty, but our dogs know that a quick snuffle can locate wads of stolen cash, illegal substances and even last night's lasagne spillage. Top perfumers would do well to employ pooch power when predicting the latest trend in whiffs, because dogs know what works, what fits and what is glaringly out of place. It's a two-pronged attack combining belly and nose, a balancing manoeuvre between intuition and scent; in essence... **if it smells right, go with it.**

Another thing our canines love is a good bottom sniff. This 'getting to know you' technique might seem overly familiar and a tad invasive to us, but it's a time-saving device allowing pups to get to the heart of the matter and establish exactly who and what they're dealing with in one swift snort. Who needs the internet when a waft of air delivers everything you need? True, only those in the doggy know are able to identify all the varying particles of information received, but it can be a life-saver, for without this kind of detail, lost and desperate hill walkers might never be tracked and found.

Be open to incoming whiffs, and trust that you and your finely tuned senses are all you need to navigate through life.

BEHOLD THE NOSE!
REVEL IN ITS GREATNESS.

Sniff Out the Good Stuff

From chicken wings to the last iced bun, dogs know how to sniff out the good stuff. To them, a shopping bag is like Santa's sack. Approach each day with the same optimistic spirit and inhale the rewards.

- **Be open to new things.**
  Change can be scary, even on a small scale. Instead of turning your nose up at something new, take a deep breath and imagine you're looking out onto an open landscape. Picture yourself stepping into this new territory. Breathe and smile!

'Memories, imagination, old sentiments, and associations are more readily reached through the SENSE OF SMELL than through any other channel.'

Oliver Wendell Holmes

- **Look for the sausages.**
  Your shopping bag could be full of sprouts, but the ever-persistent and positive mutt forages boldly on, because you never know when you're going to find a succulent morsel. In other words, be positive. Believe that life will give you the best and watch it deliver.

- **Snuffle up affection.**
  When someone gives you a compliment or shares how they feel, breathe it in. Imagine the words filling your heart with warmth, and feel that energy travel around your body until you are light and full of joy.

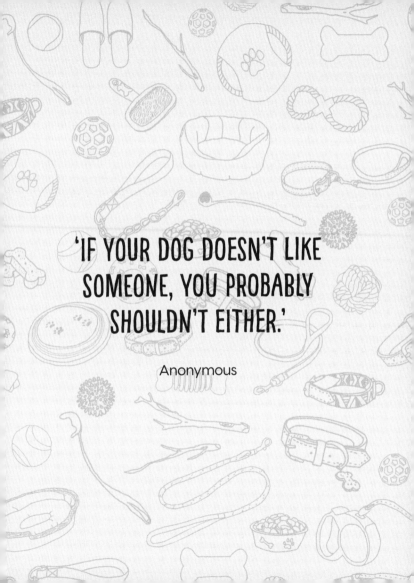

'IF YOUR DOG DOESN'T LIKE
SOMEONE, YOU PROBABLY
SHOULDN'T EITHER.'

Anonymous

Breathe With Attitude

Don't be shy when it comes to taking a breath.
Enjoy the sensation as the air hits your lungs,
giving you life and energy.

STEP ONE
Think of a scent that you like – this could
be the smell of coffee brewing, a flower or
your favourite perfume. If you can recreate
that scent physically, then do so; if not, try
to recreate the aroma in your mind.

STEP TWO
Close your eyes and imagine breathing in the
scent. Feel the joy of recognition hit you and
let the beautiful fragrance lift your spirits.

STEP THREE
Inhale, and imagine taking those feelings
of joy into your lungs.

STEP FOUR
As you exhale, imagine releasing any tension. Let the outward breath flow through you and picture it leaving your body through the soles of your feet and your fingertips.

STEP FIVE
Repeat the process, taking the joy into your lungs and letting any stress leave your body on the outward breath. Do this for five minutes every day to enhance your sense of smell and intuition, and instil inner calm.

BE MORE DOG

Pooches know what they like when it comes to an aroma. A sumptuous smell not only tickles the nose, it tweaks the tips of their ears and gets the tail wagging. Explore the world of scent and find those you love. Make a list of your favourite smells and include anything that makes you feel energised and happy – think of natural smells like flowers, plants, fruit and vegetables, and other scents like freshly washed sheets, or your mum's stew simmering in the pot. Anything goes. This is about your love of smell and how it makes you feel. When you get the chance, enjoy these scents and make them a part of your life on a regular basis.

Trust Your Senses

Being a doggy super sense, the nose acts intuitively and picks up on much more than the way something smells. While you're not gifted in this way, you can still fine-tune your intuition and work with it to identify the good, the bad and the ugly using these canine tips.

- Most intuitive feelings strike in the belly, hence the expression 'gut instinct'. Learn to identify the different sensations in your tum so that you know when something feels right, when something feels wrong, and when you're just hungry!

- When meeting people for the first time, be open and aware of how they instantly make you feel. Look at their facial expressions and body language to get a sense of how they feel, too. Practise this with friends and family, and you'll instinctively establish a connection with them and learn to read their emotions.

- The voice in your head can be your best friend or your worst critic. Inner guidance works best when you have time and space, and can silence the mind. Devote five minutes every day to breathing in peace. Close your eyes, relax and let thoughts come and go without focusing on anything. Imagine your mind is a conveyor belt and let things flow. As you practise this, you'll begin to notice the thoughts and messages that stand out and mean something.

- Test yourself. Working dogs – from those that seek out the lost to those that can smell a change in physical wellbeing – put in the hours to hone their skills. You can do the same. Simple things like guessing who's calling or texting without looking at your phone will help. The more you practise and trust your intuition, the more it will serve you.

BE MORE DOG

Pooches persist. When they sense something is wrong, they don't give up, even if the evidence isn't apparent at first glance. Be more dog and stick to your guns. Trust how you feel. You know yourself better than anyone else on the planet (apart from your canine buddy), so be true to your emotions. If in doubt, ask yourself 'What am I feeling right now? If I could put this into one word it would be...' Check in with yourself regularly for a greater sense of empowerment.

'A DOG TEACHES A BOY
FIDELITY, PERSEVERANCE,
AND TO TURN AROUND
THREE TIMES BEFORE
LYING DOWN.'

Robert Benchley

DOGGY MANTRAS

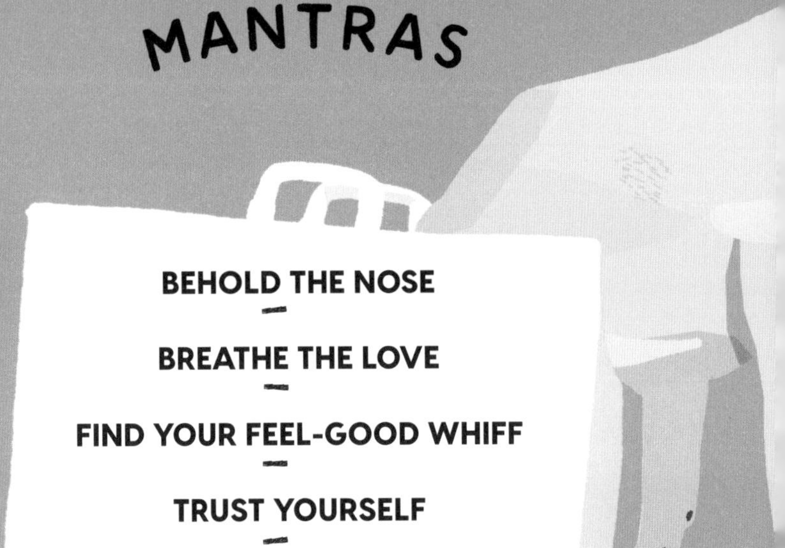
BEHOLD THE NOSE
BREATHE THE LOVE
FIND YOUR FEEL-GOOD WHIFF
TRUST YOURSELF
SMELL THE ROSES

'American dog say, "Woof, woof". Korean dog say, "Mung, mung". Polish dog say, "How, how". So which dog barking is correct? That is "human being" barking, not "dog" barking. If dog and you become one hundred per cent one, then you know sound of barking. THIS IS ZEN TEACHING. BOOM! Become one.'

Seung Sahn

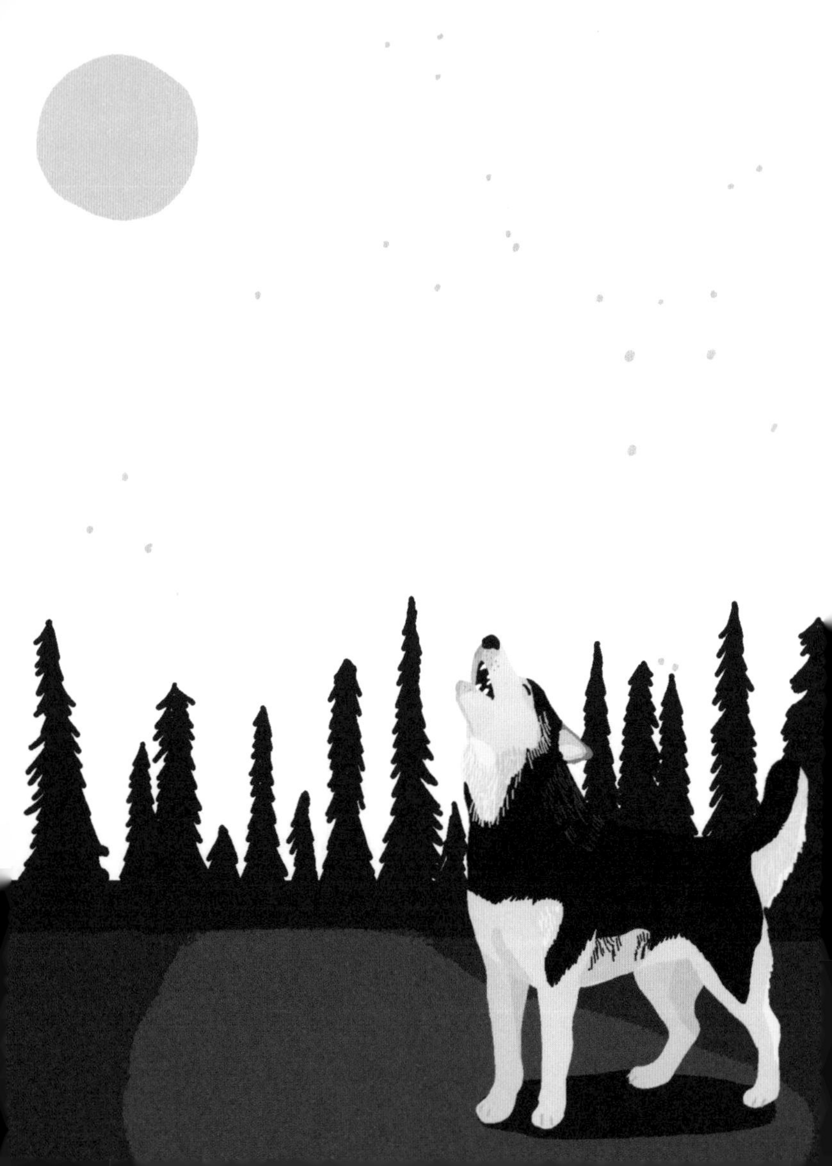

BARK
IT LOUD

Looking for a bodyguard with barkittude? Look no further. Dogs have it sussed, and while a feisty yap is usually enough to keep intruders at bay, your persevering pup will be sure to keep an alert and stoic presence by your side.

With ears like antennae and sharp, steely eyes, nothing gets past a canine. Check out Cerberus, the three-headed dog of Greek legend. It's no doubt he cut a scary figure. They say three heads are better than one, and with triple the snarling jaws he made the perfect guardian to the gates of the Underworld. Slippery souls seeking solace found puppy love in short supply from this hungry hound.

Stand up for yourself and your pack, that's the doggy ethos. Get attention when it counts, and if in doubt **bark it loud and proud**. Meek mewling is not the way of the super mutt.

When it comes to guarding duties, you cannot be shy with your yowl. It comes from the fiery pit of your tum and enters the world in a shower of spittle. A hit in the face has more grace, but the bark says, 'Hey dude, pay attention, NOW!' No messing, no faffing.

Protection is an instinct that runs deep in the veins of every pooch.

From the teeniest Chihuahua pup to the lumbering might of the St Bernard, dogs do defence. It comes from a place of love, and our caring canines are always on the lookout for new ways to show affection, whether as an extra pair of eyes, at our side as we pad through the day, or as ears, pricked up and ready to jump to it. These leaping lovelies are happy to serve, making us feel on top of the world and secure in their company. Even newborn babes are bow-wow blessed; a fervent lick to the face covers all the bases according to folklore, ensuring the child is quick to heal from illness and injury as they grow. What's not to love?

The Ancients knew best. In Mesoamerican culture the dog was seen as the ultimate guardian and protector, carrying the souls of the dead to their final resting place. No surprise then that the people of Chupícuaro were often buried with their trusty hounds to ensure they would reach the next life safely and with a faithful friend at their side.

WHETHER ESCORTING, DEFENDING, DIVINING OR DEFYING THE ODDS, OUR MULTI-TASKING POOCHES DO IT ALL WITH A PRIDE AND LOVE THAT MAKES THEM STAND OUT FROM THE REST.

Unleash your barkittude

Find your stride and feel an overwhelming
sense of purpose and power with these five top
tips straight from the mutt's lips.

1 **Know what and who counts in your life.**
Every day, list three things that matter, three
things you'd like to achieve and three people
you want to thank for their presence in your
world. Keep these lists in mind as you go

about your business and try to reach the goals you've outlined. Tick off any targets you achieve at the end of the day.

2 Get yappy and give yourself a pep talk.
It's easy to fall foul of doubt and lose confidence, but keep things in perspective. Tell yourself you're doing good by repeating positive affirmations throughout the day.

Simple statements like 'I can do this' or 'Every step I take, I move forwards' will motivate and keep you on track.

3 **Bark out compliments not orders.**
   Be kind and encouraging when dealing
   with others. Let people know you appreciate
   them with a 'thank you' and a smile.

4 **Talk a tall tale.**
   Instead of focusing on the negative and
   imagining the worst-case scenario, get
   canine creative and see the best. In a couple
   of sentences tell a simple story of what you'd
   like to happen and how you'd like events to
   pan out. Read the story out loud, as if you're
   telling it to an audience. Inject energy and
   passion into the tale and try to picture a
   positive outcome.

5 **Play around with words.**
   Poetry might not be your thing, but words
   have power. Write rhyming quotes and
   pin them around the house on mirrors,
   noticeboards and fridges. Things like **feel the
   real deal** or **vanquish the dark with your bark**!
   Take inspiration from the Doggy Mantras in
   this book and use them as prompts to switch
   up the way you're feeling.

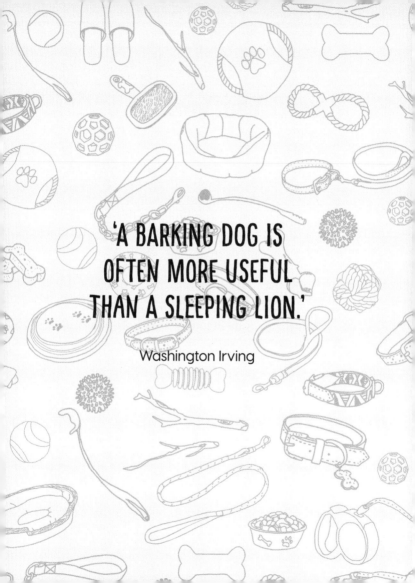

'A BARKING DOG IS
OFTEN MORE USEFUL
THAN A SLEEPING LION.'

Washington Irving

Howl Your Yowl

Barking at the moon, or at the long-suffering postman, might be a step too far for us, but there's something to be said for an old-fashioned belly bellow. There are many ways to howl your yowl and feel good to the bone!

STEP ONE
List three songs that you love to sing along to. Try to pick upbeat tracks with lots of energy and volume.

STEP TWO
Make sure you won't be disturbed, and that you're not likely to disturb anyone else. Stick on some comfortable clothing and make some space to move.

STEP THREE
Get the tracks lined up and ready to play. If
you want to warm up first, you can play a few
other tunes and get used to singing along.

STEP FOUR
Stick on your tracks of choice and raise your
voice. Imagine you're centre stage, with an
audience of adoring fans, and sing as loud
as you can. Get lost in the music and allow
yourself to move freely and with feeling!

'THE TREE LOOKS LIKE A DOG,
BARKING AT HEAVEN.'

Jack Kerouac

BE
MORE
DOG

There's nothing more infectious than an enthusiastic yap, especially when it's coupled with a fervent spring, two fluffy paws and a wet nose pushed triumphantly in your face. We express our joy in more reserved ways, but that doesn't mean we can't get equally animated. Your laugh is your yap. Use it with passion. Feel the first tremors in your belly, take a deep breath and let it vibrate through your chest with force. Practise laughing in front of the mirror; as daft as it sounds, you'll feel the mood-enhancing effects almost immediately.

Bow-wow Blessings

Dogs are always searching for new ways to show they care. Tireless in their need to support, guide and be at our side, they always find a way to touch the heart. Follow their lead and share bow-wow blessings aplenty!

- Pin your ears back and get used to listening to others. This means giving them time and space to talk, share their views and express how they feel.

- Use your puppy peepers and pay close attention to the people who matter. Check out their body language, and if you see someone struggling, lend a hand.

- Surprise friends and family by taking them out for a walk. Go somewhere you've never been before so that you can explore it together and create fun memories.

- Be by the side of your loved ones in times of trouble and in times of joy. Be a strong, silent presence that they can rely on.

- Don't shy away from speaking up. If you see that someone is suffering, or having a hard time of it, say something. Be the voice of reason, and should they need it, their voice when they can't find the words to express how they feel. **Be the voice they can rely upon, come what may.**

BE MORE DOG

Keep your senses canine crisp by exercising them regularly. Go outside on a blustery day and stand facing the wind. Feel the way it tugs at your skin and rushes through your hair. Notice how it smells and tastes as you take in deep breaths. Feel it buffeting against you, making your body sway gently, and be aware of how this makes you feel inside. Take this a step further and run into the wind. Let it carry you forwards as it presses against your skin. Take in deep breaths and enjoy dancing with the elements!

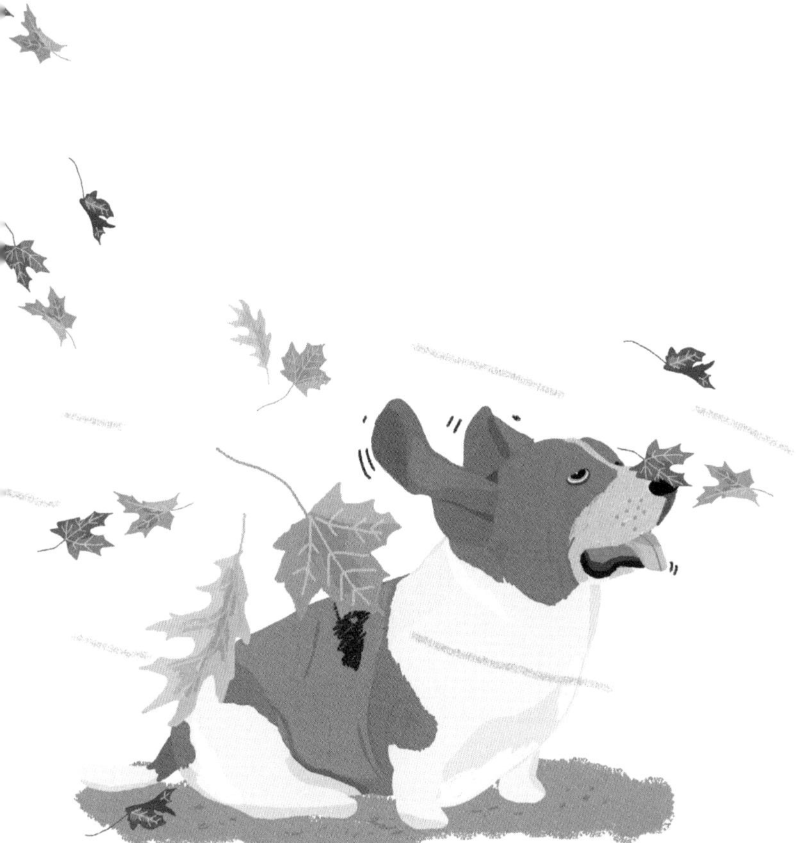

DOGGY MANTRAS

JUMP TO IT

—

HOWL YOUR YOWL

—

LEAP WITH LOVE

—

LIVE – LOVE – BARK

—

BE YAPPY HAPPY!

'The dogs did bark, the children screamed, up flew the windows all; And every soul bawled out, WELL DONE! As loud as he could bawl.'

William Cowper

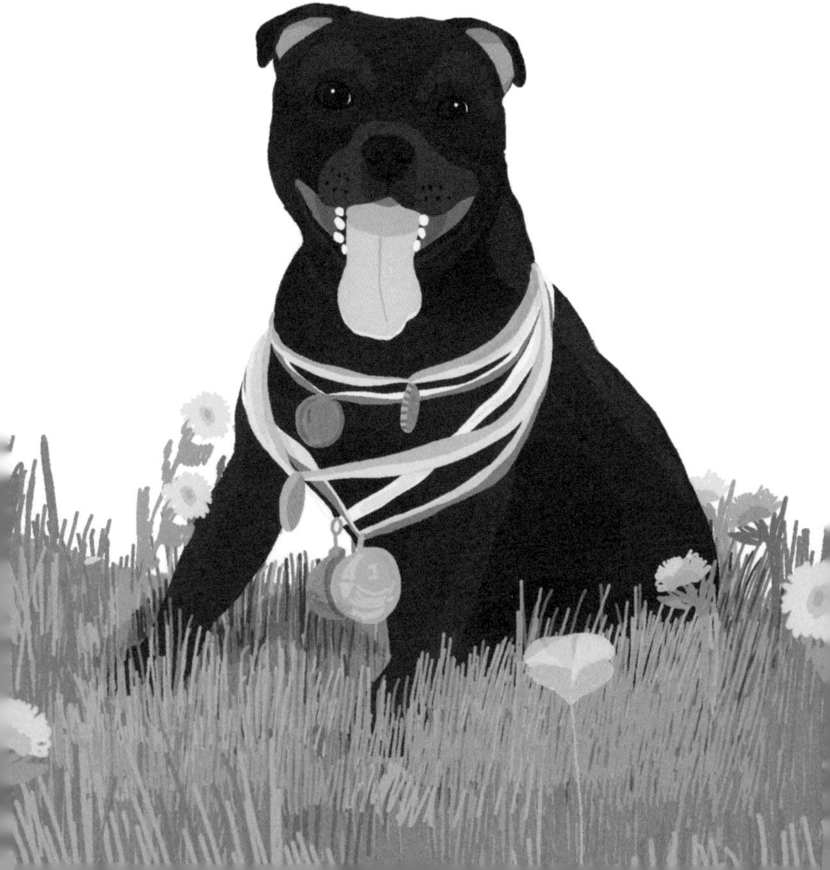

BE YOUR OWN TOP DOG

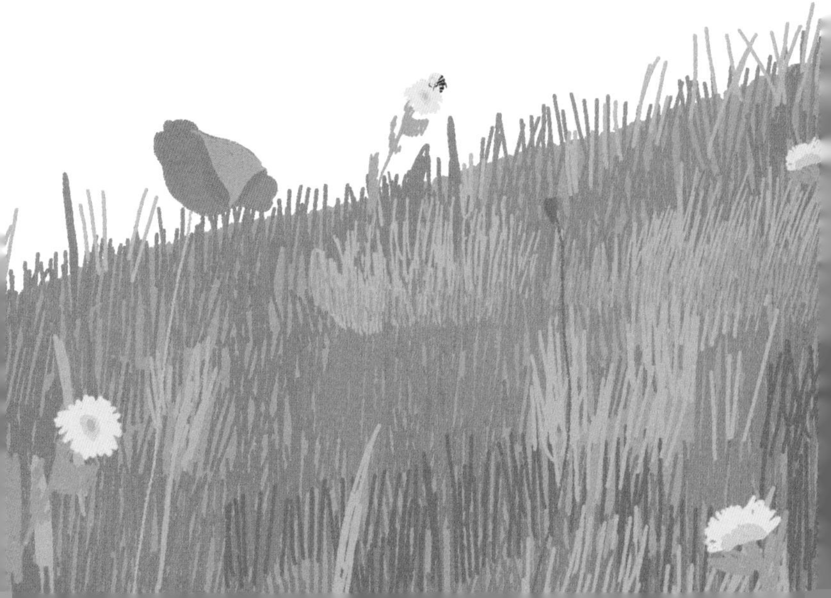

In poochville, there's no one-size-fits-all. From large and lumbering to svelte and uber chic, dogs embrace diversity.

Whether cute and fluffy morsels of perfection or strapping muscular beings of beauty, dogs are unique and ready to slot into our lives (and our handbags) should we require it. There's no such thing as the underdog, because every pup has something to offer. Need a gentle companion to share sloppy cuddles on the sofa? Check. A super-fast running buddy to keep you on your toes and reaching those fitness goals? Check. Everything can be ticked off the list because **nothing is impossible in the world of dog**.

And while talents aren't always obvious or reasonable (goofing around may seem surplus to requirements, but over time, canine capers are the best antidote to a challenging day in the office), they will be revealed in due course. From making patterns in the snow with their belly, to saving water by offering refreshing wet fur showers, our pooches utilise their differences to bring us a daily dose of doggy delightfulness.

There's no one-muttmanship on this block, only shared joy, because life is great when you accept who you are and what you have to offer.

Like a giant canine jigsaw puzzle, there's a perfect fit in life and love for everyone. **TOP DOG** may be a title worth having, but it doesn't matter how high a dog can jump or cock its leg, when there's a bottom worth sniffing they'll be there in a heartbeat, because that's who they are and what they do. This healthy self-acceptance carries through to us too, which is why all bets are off when puppy dog eyes are turned on. Who can resist the look of love? Unique, complete and truly special, it's all about the differences, the one-of-a-kind idiosyncrasies that match human to canine and vice versa. Every family has a fit, a canine-shaped hole waiting to be filled, just as in life, everyone has their place.

THAT'S GOT TO BE WORTH A WOOF IN ANYONE'S BOOK!

Define Your Differences

What makes you special? If you struggle to answer this question, then it's time to define your differences with a little canine help.

STEP ONE
Make a list of things you enjoy doing, from chatting with friends to taking a walk in the sunshine. If you find this difficult, start at the beginning of each day and go through your usual routine, finding the things you like to do.

STEP TWO
Make a list of things you're good at. Ask friends and family to contribute their thoughts. They will often highlight things you hadn't considered.

STEP THREE
Make a list of any quirky traits you have. This includes habits, likes, interests and things that you hold dear.

STEP FOUR

Read through each list and you'll begin to see how fabulous and unique you are. Circle three things from each list that stand out and are more important to you than the rest.

STEP FIVE

Examine your top choices and see if you can combine them in some way. For example, you might enjoy cleaning and tidying, and you might have a talent for communication and an interest in vlogging. Put them together and perhaps you could turn your hand to creating a series of vlogs on how to maximise space and clear the clutter.

STEP SIX

Consider how you can use your skills and talents in a productive way, and have fun at the same time!

STEP SEVEN

Keep adding to the list. You'll find that as you focus on the things you enjoy and are good at, you'll notice even more attributes and skills you can use.

Five doses of doggy delightfulness

1 Do, don't dally.
Dogs don't spend their precious time lost in thought or worry. They throw themselves into things with gusto. If there's something you'd like to do, that you enjoy doing and that makes you feel special, just do it!

2 Be yourself, not someone else.
Don't try to copy or compete with others. Our pooches may be competitive in spirit, but while the pug might strive to win the race, he doesn't pretend he's a greyhound to get there!

3 It's OK to be silly, to stand out from the crowd and have fun.
Even the most fashion-forward pooch is prepared to fly in the face of decorum and muddy their best coat, if there's joy to be had.

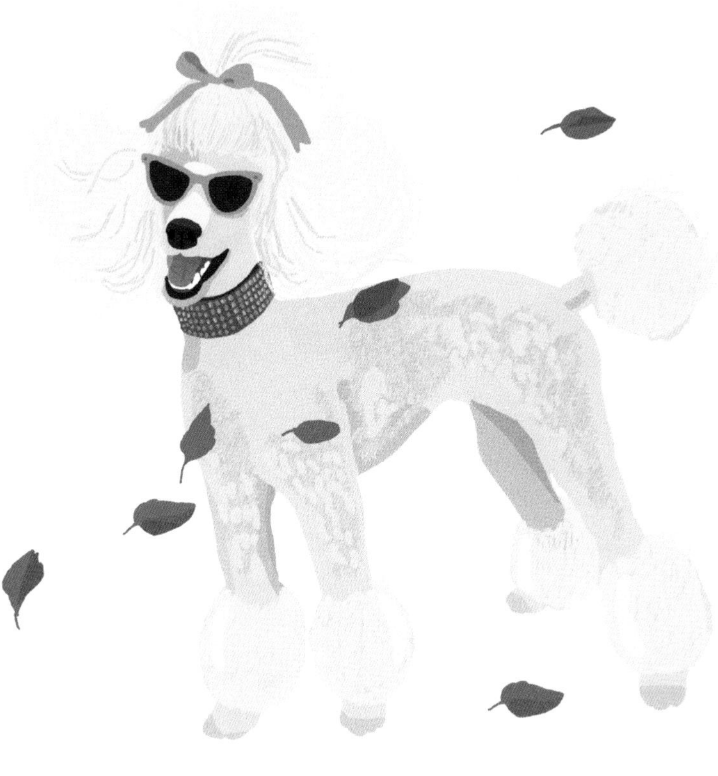

4 **Go the whole dog.**
It doesn't matter what you do, do it 100 per cent. If you don't succeed, at least you tried and experienced life. There's always another day, another race, another chance for a sweet bite of the biscuit.

5 **The things you hate can turn out to be the things you love.**
At first glance, apple slices aren't as tempting as freshly grilled burgers, but add a dollop of peanut butter and they can be a godsend when the canine munchies strike. In other words, your wacky dance moves might not bring you street cred, but they could get you noticed by the love of your life!

BE
MORE
DOG

Once you've created your canine haven, be sure to use it. Dogs take regular naps and enjoy relaxing with those they love. Follow suit and take time out every day to sit, breathe and recharge. Put your feet up, close your eyes and focus on each breath. Slow down the pace of your breathing and let any thoughts float in and out of your mind.

BE MORE DOG

Howl out your praises. Pick one thing each day from your list of skills and put it into a positive affirmation. For example, if you're good at cooking, you might say, 'I cook sumptuous meals to nourish my body and mind every day!' Say it out loud morning and night, and repeat it in your head as you go about your business.

'IF A DOG WILL NOT COME
TO YOU AFTER HAVING
LOOKED YOU IN THE FACE,
YOU SHOULD GO HOME AND
EXAMINE YOUR CONSCIENCE.'

Woodrow Wilson

Find Your Furry Fit

There's nothing like that cosy spot on the sofa – prime position for the pooch who loves to snooze in comfort in front of the TV. For some, it's a super-soft cushion delicately perfumed by themselves; for others, it's a basket with their favourite snuggly blanket and foodie treats within pawing distance. It's different for every dog, but it's always just right; the perfect fit, and a place where a pup can be at peace and at one with the world.

Create your own canine haven with these top dog tips, and make it a space where you can recharge and unwind.

- Go for comfort and texture when choosing furnishings and accessories. Think soft and fluffy fabrics that you want to touch and feel next to your skin. Opt for warm throws, snuggly cushions and lots of luxurious layers.

- Choose colours that remind you of the great outdoors. Beautiful sky blues, gentle cloud-like creams and the muted browns and pinks of the earth make you feel secure and calm.

- Images of dogs at play or rest will inspire a sense of fun and adventure, and remind you to live in the moment.

- Smell is uber important, as any dog worth his bacon will affirm. Burn scented candles and oils to create a soothing atmosphere. Go for lavender, sandalwood, geranium and rose to bring the outside in, and promote peace and wellbeing.

DOGGY MANTRAS

DOGS DIG DIVERSITY

—

YOU FIT PERFECTLY

—

GO THE WHOLE DOG

—

FIND YOUR POOCH POWER

—

ACCEPT YOUR FURRY-SELF

'A dog is the only thing on earth that LOVES YOU MORE than he loves himself.'

Josh Billings

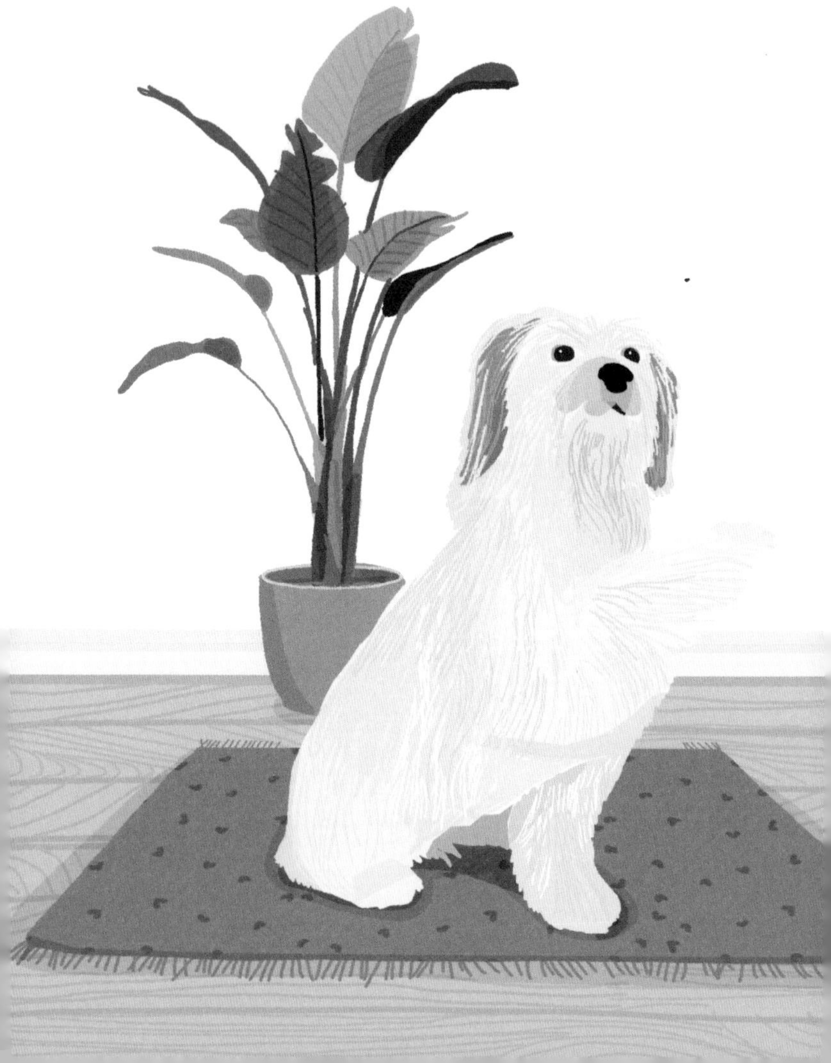

THE
POWER OF
THE PAW

You cannot fail to smile in the presence of a pooch. Whether sniffing your shoe, offering a muddy paw or nuzzling close for a dribble-laden kiss, there's no denying the power of puppy love.

Dogs deliver devotion in many ways. Their eagerness to please knows no bounds, as they go above and beyond the call of duty to plant a smile firmly on the face of everyone they encounter. The truth is, dogs have a short-term memory of around three seconds, which means they forgive and forget in a heartbeat, making canine grudges and any other such grievance pretty much non-existent. Their open and loving hearts

are ready to give, give, give in one gentle stroke. It's a natural process with no real effort involved; it's hardwired into doggy DNA.

Love just is, and dogs just are. Enough said.

The power of the paw is a curious thing, for where we might tire of lending a hand, and secretly hope for something in return, the considerate canine has no ulterior motive. It is driven by a need to please, and the sheer delight that comes with genuine affection. Whether playing fetch the ball, catch the frisbee or present the slipper, the joy is always in the giving.

Kindness has its own reward, and a playful pat on the back is worth more than any gift, human or otherwise. It says 'You're mine and I'm yours. We understand each other, we're a team.' It's enough to make any doggy diva stand on furry tippy toes and bark with glee!

Lending a paw is about going the extra mile for a smile, and not giving a biscuit bone about it. If it turns the frown upside down, that's all that counts.

To be enthused and ready to please, come what may, is to be DOG with a capital D.

'KINDNESS IS THE LANGUAGE
THAT THE DEAF CAN HEAR
AND THE BLIND CAN SEE.'

Mark Twain

Find Your Paw Power

When we do something for someone else it lifts
two hearts: ours and theirs. Dogs understand
this simple truth and practise it every day. You
can do the same. Choose at least one thing
from this list each day to make someone smile.

Be courteous.
Open a door for someone else.

Be patient.
Stand back and let a stranger get on the bus
or train before you.

Carry shopping.
You could offer to shop for elderly neighbours,
friends and family, or just assist someone who
is struggling with heavy bags.

Strike up a conversation.
Whatever you're doing, there are always
plenty of opportunities to get talking to
someone new. At the most, you'll make
a friend, and at the least, you'll brighten
someone's day.

Pay it forwards.
Buy the next person in the queue a morning coffee, then watch as the kindness multiplies.

Feed the soul.
Bake a cake, then share it with friends and colleagues.

Offer words of encouragement.
If someone's not feeling their best or having a bad day, show some understanding and help to reassure them that everything will be OK.

Give someone flowers.
They don't have to be expensive; a pretty bunch from your garden has the same effect as designer blooms.

Volunteer your services.
You could do something for charity, or simply offer to help in other ways, from gardening to walking the pooch.

Take a step back.
Life can often be a rush. Everyone has their own agenda. Take a step back and give people time and space rather than piling the pressure on. It will help you feel calmer too!

Show the Love

When we're happy and secure we feel more loving towards others, so if you want to show the love, the best place to start is with yourself. Cultivate an air of self-acceptance, and you'll be keen to show others how much you care.

1 Stand in front of a full-length mirror.

2 Adjust your posture so you're standing tall with your shoulders back.

3 Imagine there's a thread travelling up your spine and emerging from the top of your head. Feel it gently tugging upwards to lengthen your body.

4 Gaze at your reflection, taking in every part of your body and noticing how it fits together perfectly.

5 Consider each body part, how it works and what it does for you every day.

6 Look yourself in the eye and give thanks for the miracle that is you.

7 Repeat at least once a day to reaffirm the love.

'If I could be HALF the person my dog is, I'd be TWICE the human I am.'

Charles Yu

BE
MORE
DOG

There's nothing a dog enjoys more than a good nuzzle, and they certainly don't skimp on the love. Our canines appreciate the power of touch and understand that it goes a long way to making people feel safe and accepted. Whether it's a simple tap of the arm, a quick embrace or a full-on rib-cracker of a hug, reaching out in a non-threatening way speaks volumes. Give hugs freely and you'll also reap the benefits by boosting levels of oxytocin.

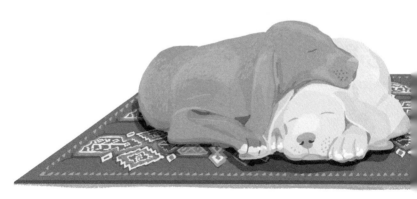

Nudge the Grudge

Got a grievance that still makes you growl? It might not be easy to forget, but you can learn to let go and release the pain. Make your heart lighter and your outlook brighter with this step-by-step exercise.

STEP ONE
Light a candle to create a soothing atmosphere. Burn lavender-scented oil to promote peace and inner calm.

STEP TWO
Take a piece of paper and write everything down. If it's a person that's upset you, write down what they did and how it made you feel. If it's a situation, outline it and include any emotions.

STEP THREE
Fold the letter up and hold it in your hands.
Close your eyes and slow your breathing.

STEP FOUR
Say, 'I let this go. I release it. I am free.'

STEP FIVE
Open your eyes and pass the letter through
the flame of the candle, then let it burn to ash
in a fireproof dish.

STEP SIX
Take the ashes outside and scatter them. As
you do so, repeat the affirmation, 'I let this go.
I release it. I am free.'

BE
MORE
DOG

Dogs win friends and admirers because they don't hold back. They'll shower you with kisses and show they're pleased to see you, even when you're having a bad day. Your face may say 'go away', but that's just an open invitation to kill you with kindness, and it works! Follow suit and turn on the charm. When faced with a difficult person or situation, instead of reciprocating anger or frustration, go out of your way to be kind. Spread your smile even wider and say, 'What can I do to make things better?'

'To err is human – to FORGIVE, canine.'

Anonymous

DOGGY MANTRAS

**WHEN YOU'RE PAWSOME,
YOU'RE AWESOME**

—

ATTACK WITH KINDNESS

—

GIVE, GIVE, GIVE!

—

NUDGE THE GRUDGE

—

BE TEAM 'EVERYONE'

'The BOND with
a true dog is as
lasting as the
ties of this earth
will ever be.'

Konrad Lorenz

Managing Director Sarah Lavelle
Editorial Director Harriet Butt
Editor Harriet Webster
Editorial Assistant Ellie Spence
Designer Nicola Ellis
Cover Designer Alicia House
Illustrator Hanna Melin
Head of Production Stephen Lang
Production Controller Martina
Georgieva

Originally published in 2019 by
Quadrille Publishing Limited

This edition published in 2024 by
Quadrille Publishing Limited

Quadrille
52–54 Southwark Street
London SE1 1UN
quadrille.com

Cataloguing in Publication Data:
a catalogue record for this book
is available from the British Library.

Text © Alison Davies 2024
Illustrations © Hanna Melin 2024
Design © Quadrille 2024

ISBN 978 1 83783 265 1

Printed in China using vegetable-
based inks

MIX
Paper | Supporting
responsible forestry
FSC
www.fsc.org   FSC® C018179

'The BOND with a true dog is as lasting as the ties of this earth will ever be.'

Konrad Lorenz

Managing Director Sarah Lavelle
Editorial Director Harriet Butt
Editor Harriet Webster
Editorial Assistant Ellie Spence
Designer Nicola Ellis
Cover Designer Alicia House
Illustrator Hanna Melin
Head of Production Stephen Lang
Production Controller Martina
Georgieva

Originally published in 2019 by
Quadrille Publishing Limited

This edition published in 2024 by
Quadrille Publishing Limited

Quadrille
52–54 Southwark Street
London SE1 1UN
quadrille.com

MIX
Paper | Supporting
responsible forestry
FSC
www.fsc.org FSC® C018179

Cataloguing in Publication Data:
a catalogue record for this book
is available from the British Library.

Text © Alison Davies 2024
Illustrations © Hanna Melin 2024
Design © Quadrille 2024

ISBN 978 1 83783 265 1

Printed in China using vegetable-
based inks